THIS ORGANIZER
BELONGS TO:

LAST UPDATED ON _____

AFTER I'M GONE

ORGANIZER

A Simple Journal about My Affairs & Last Wishes

JOSHUA P. GIBBONS, ESQ.

CONTENTS

INTRODUCTION

The following planner was designed to help you get your affairs in order, both for yourself and for your loved ones. It's a valuable, all-in-one resource for your whats, whys, and wishes when you can no longer share that information. Planning ahead for your passing may feel uncomfortable, emotional, or even confusing, but it's critical to provide loved ones with clear communication so they can have peace of mind settling your affairs, knowing what they're doing is in line with your hopes and intentions.

Once completed, this planner will contain information on all facets of your life, including additional pages for the aspects unique to you. Given your specific life needs, you may not need to use every space or section of this book, but I have attempted to include some of the most important items for a variety of situations, such as your personal wishes, security information, financial planning, health information, and other everyday matters.

After filling out this organizer, be sure to store it in a secure location, such as a safe or deposit box, as it will contain highly sensitive information. Please share its location with your lawyer and any family member or representatives who would need access to this information, ideally with any other important documents that would also be needed (i.e., your official will and other legal documents). Just as you may update your will with important changes from time to time, I recommend revisiting this planner once a year in case any information or wishes have changed.

This planner also contains references and information about a few other types of legal documents to help make any end-of-life decisions easier for your loved ones. It is important to note that all this information is generalized, and every state and country has its own specific requirements governing such documents. It's important to consider getting individualized legal guidance and/or pursuing state-specific research for whichever documents or directives are appropriate for you, especially to ensure you have enacted your wishes in the manner required by where you live.

To that end, it is vital to know that **this document is not a will and is not in any way to be considered a legal document**. A will is a legal document that will memorialize your last wishes and what you would like to happen with your possessions after you are gone. While I am an attorney, I crafted this not from the perspective of drafting a specific legal document, but to help organize your thoughts when thinking about the end of your life and all the other important details that come with estate planning. Shortly after I passed the bar, when preparing end-of-life documents for family and friends, I was struck by how many items are truly not considered when creating your own plans. Consequently, this planner provides details on a variety of personal information including details about your possessions, but **any instructions given herein are not legally binding.**

If you already have a will, it is important to ensure it is up to date. If an outdated will has not been officially revoked according to your state's laws, it will remain intact *regardless* of how out of date it may be, and ***in no circumstances would this planner be considered a replacement for that will***.

Note to loved ones reading this planner: This organizer will help you find important information about my life and navigate next steps after I'm gone. It's organized with the most basic information you'll need and will move to more in-depth sections, but feel free to jump to specific topics you may need. You may wish to start with the "What to Do When I Pass Away" section on page 19.

PERSONAL INFORMATION

NAME _____

FULL LEGAL NAME _____

_____

Also known as (*Nicknames, maiden names, etc.*) _____

_____

BIRTH DATE AND BIRTHPLACE (*Refer to Important Documents*)

_____

_____

_____

SOCIAL SECURITY NUMBER

_____

ADDRESS (*Refer to Personal Property*) _____

_____

_____

P.O. BOX NUMBER _____

P.O. box key is located _____

PHONE NUMBER(S) _____

_____

FAMILY

MARRIED/PARTNERSHIP STATUS _____

Partner's name and contact information

_____

_____

_____

_____

Children's names and contact information

_____   _____

_____   _____

_____   _____

_____   _____

_____   _____

_____   _____

_____   _____

_____   _____

_____   _____

_____   _____

Grandchildren's names and contact information

_____   _____

_____   _____

_____   _____

_____   _____

_____   _____

_____   _____

_____   _____

_____   _____

_____   _____

_____   _____

_____   _____

_____   _____

_____   _____

_____   _____

_____   _____

_____   _____

Previous marriages/partners' names and contact information

_____   _____

_____   _____

_____   _____

_____   _____

_____   _____

Siblings' names and contact information

_____   _____

_____   _____

_____   _____

_____   _____

_____   _____

_____   _____

_____   _____

_____   _____

_____   _____

Parents' names and birthplaces

_____   _____

_____   _____

_____   _____

_____   _____

_____   _____

PERSONAL AND PROFESSIONAL

CAREER _____

_____

_____

_____

_____

HOBBIES AND AFFILIATIONS _____

_____

_____

_____

AWARDS AND ACCOMPLISHMENTS _____

_____

_____

BELIEFS AND VALUES _____

_____

_____

COMMUNITY INVOLVEMENT _____

_____

_____

_____

_____

CITIZENSHIP _____

_____

_____

_____

_____

RELIGIOUS BELIEFS AND ORGANIZATIONS _____

_____

_____

_____

_____

MILITARY SERVICE _____

_____

_____

_____

_____

Notes

KEY CONTACT INFORMATION

This section is designed for any key contacts to whom you want your loved ones to reach out, rather than a full contact listing of your community, friends, or family. Think of this as a list of everyone who will be assisting those responsible for carrying out your wishes. Of course, if there is anyone else who is critically important, you should include them as well.

EXECUTOR:

CONTACT INFORMATION

_____

_____

_____

ATTORNEY:

CONTACT INFORMATION

_____

_____

_____

ACCOUNTANT:

CONTACT INFORMATION

_____

_____

_____

TAX PREPARER:

CONTACT INFORMATION

_____

_____

_____

FINANCIAL ADVISOR:

CONTACT INFORMATION

_____

_____

_____

INSURANCE AGENT:

CONTACT INFORMATION

_____

_____

_____

PRIMARY CARE PHYSICIAN:

CONTACT INFORMATION

_____

_____

_____

HEALTH CARE PROVIDER(S):

CONTACT INFORMATION

_____

_____

_____

CLERGYPERSON:

CONTACT INFORMATION

_____

_____

_____

OTHER:

CONTACT INFORMATION

_____

_____

_____

MEDICAL INFORMATION

This section is designed for you to consider what happens in cases of medical urgency and necessity, when you are no longer able to communicate said decisions on your own. Be it the medication you are on, your blood type and allergies, or who will be making medical decisions on your behalf, it is prudent to consider what you would like others to know before you no longer have the chance to share that information.

It may be prudent to consider a Do Not Resuscitate (DNR) Order, a living will, and/or a healthcare power of attorney. A DNR can be created by informing your doctor and healthcare team of your wishes, and if you desire one, relay that in your living will or healthcare power of attorney document.

A living will is a very specific document used to outline your desires if you develop a terminal condition or permanent incapacitation and only applies to these types of situations. Your living will can outline whether you want death-delaying procedures.

A healthcare power of attorney allows you to appoint a selected agent to make your healthcare decisions when you are incapacitated, even temporarily. You can grant your agent as broad or limited discretion for making such decisions as you would like. If you recover from your condition, you will again be able to make your own healthcare decisions.

These directives can all be kept separate if desired or can all be incorporated into a healthcare power of attorney.

LIVING WILL LOCATION *(Refer to Important Documents)*

HEALTHCARE POWER OF ATTORNEY LOCATION

(Refer to Important Documents)

Appointed agent and contact information _____

_____

_____

DNR LOCATION *(Refer to Important Documents)*

ORGAN DONATION LOCATION

BLOOD TYPE _____

MEDICAL CONDITIONS

MEDICATIONS

_____

_____

_____

_____

_____

ALLERGIES AND REACTIONS _____

_____

_____

_____

HEALTH INSURANCE INFORMATION _____

_____

_____

_____

HEALTH INSURANCE CARD LOCATION

PRIMARY CARE PHYSICIAN _(Refer to Key Contacts)_

_____

_____

_____

OTHER PHYSICIANS *(Refer to Key Contacts)*

_____   _____

_____   _____

_____   _____

_____   _____

_____   _____

_____   _____

_____   _____

_____   _____

_____   _____

_____   _____

_____   _____

_____   _____

_____   _____

_____   _____

_____   _____

PREFERRED HOSPITAL _____

Location and contact information

PREFERRED PHARMACY _____

Location and contact information

Things to do if I'm temporarily incapacitated _____

_____

_____

_____

_____

_____

_____

_____

_____

_____

_____

_____

_____

_____

_____

_____

WHAT TO DO
WHEN I PASS AWAY

This section outlines specific information that will be immediately necessary at the time of your passing. Each piece of information you provide below can be used by your loved ones to take the immediate next steps after you are gone. This includes ensuring family is contacted and plans are made to say goodbye in a manner you wish.

For loved ones: First, it is recommended that eight to twelve copies of the death certificate be requested from the doctor or funeral director. Death certificates are primarily not accepted when photocopied or photographed and are needed to close out the variety of accounts in an individual's name, such as insurance, Social Security, bank accounts, pensions, 401(k) plans, IRS, credit cards, and some utilities. The information found throughout this book should provide a good benchmark for how many copies are needed, but it is always wise to secure a few more than you think.

Please contact the following people upon my death:

FAMILY MEMBERS:

CONTACT INFORMATION

_____

_____

_____

_____

FRIENDS:

CONTACT INFORMATION

_____

_____

_____

_____

EMPLOYER:

CONTACT INFORMATION

_____

_____

_____

MILITARY, IF APPLICABLE:

CONTACT INFORMATION

_____

_____

FUNERAL ARRANGEMENTS

If you have any specific desires for what loved ones should do while organizing your funeral service and your preferred final resting place (e.g., burial, cremation, etc.), outline them here. Be as specific or general as you'd like (for example: What type of memorial, wake, or ceremony would you like? What type of music, religious details, photos, etc., would you want shared?)

INSURANCE POLICY FOR FUNERAL/BURIAL EXPENSES

_____

_____

_____

_____

_____

_____

HOW I WOULD LIKE MY REMAINS HANDLED _____

_____

_____

_____

_____

_____

_____

_____

CEMETERY BURIAL _____

_____

_____

_____

_____

_____

MEMORIAL STONE _____

_____

_____

_____

_____

_____

CREMATION _____

_____

_____

_____

_____

_____

OTHER _____

_____

_____

_____

_____

FUNERAL HOME _____

_____

_____

_____

_____

FUNERAL WISHES AND OTHER ARRANGEMENTS _____

_____

_____

_____

_____

_____

_____

OBITUARY INFORMATION _____

_____

_____

_____

_____

_____

_____

_____

_____

INFORMATION ABOUT MY DEPENDENTS

_____

Dependents are, as the name suggests, family members who depend on you for care and financial support. When outlining your dependents' information, keep in mind the goal of this section is to capture anything that will assist a future guardian or custodian in providing the necessary type of care for these individuals. While financial matters and specific care logistics (such as who future guardians would be) may be noted in your will, this section aims to provide details that would otherwise not be captured, such as information about conditions or allergies.

NAME:

RELATIONSHIP _____

BIRTH DATE AND PLACE _____

_____

CITIZENSHIP _____

OTHER PERSONAL INFORMATION _____

_____

_____

_____

CAREGIVING, CUSTODY, OR GUARDIANSHIP INFORMATION

_____

_____

_____

Location of documents

HEALTH AND MEDICAL INFORMATION _____

_____

_____

_____

CONDITIONS   ## ALLERGIES

_____   _____

_____   _____

_____   _____

_____

HEALTHCARE PROVIDERS

_____   _____

_____   _____

_____   _____

_____   _____

26

HEALTH INSURANCE INFORMATION _____

_____

_____

_____

```
Location of documents



```

NOTES AND INSTRUCTIONS FOR CARE _____

_____

_____

_____

NAME:

RELATIONSHIP _____

BIRTH DATE AND PLACE _____

_____

CITIZENSHIP _____

OTHER PERSONAL INFORMATION _____

_____

_____

_____

_____

CAREGIVING, CUSTODY, OR GUARDIANSHIP INFORMATION

_____

_____

_____

Location of documents

HEALTH AND MEDICAL INFORMATION _____

_____

_____

_____

CONDITIONS

_____

_____

_____

_____

ALLERGIES

_____

_____

_____

_____

HEALTHCARE PROVIDERS

_____

_____

_____

_____

_____

_____

_____

_____

HEALTH INSURANCE INFORMATION _____

_____

_____

_____

Location of documents

NOTES AND INSTRUCTIONS FOR CARE _____

_____

_____

_____

_____

_____

_____

_____

_____

_____

_____

FINANCIAL INFORMATION

The following section has financial and monetary details that are important for your loved ones to know about so they can get a handle on your finances, pay bills, and close any of your accounts. The more information you can provide below, the easier it will be to resolve your estate. However, as you are outlining private information in detail, I will take this opportunity to remind you to store this book somewhere secure.

In addition to specific financial documents, it may be prudent to consider granting a power of attorney. A power of attorney is an important document for planning purposes and is distinct from a healthcare power of attorney (discussed in the *Medical Information* section). To keep things clear, you can consider a power of attorney as a financial power of attorney.

A financial power of attorney document grants a selected agent the power to make financial decisions on your behalf while you are alive. The financial power of attorney can be as broad or as limited as you desire and can impact real estate holding, finances, etc. In the document, you can grant an individual (or individuals) the right to make any financial decisions on your behalf, such as selling property, opening bank accounts, or any other such power you would like to bestow.

A financial power of attorney will end upon mental incapacitation unless stated otherwise. Therefore, if you want your financial power of attorney to continue during incapacitation, you should create a durable power of attorney. Alternatively, if you do not want someone to have power over financial decisions until you become incapacitated, you can create a springing power of attorney, which will only go into effect when you lose capacity to make certain decisions (which you can define).

Finally, you can retract a power of attorney at any time either by writing a revocation of said power of attorney, destroying all copies of the existing power of attorney, or creating a new power of attorney. Consequently, it is important to always keep track of any such forms you create.

Upon death, the financial power of attorney will no longer be effective, regardless of type, and such decision-making power will be transferred either to the executor of the will or, if there is no will, to an administrator appointed by the probate court.

FINANCIAL POWER OF ATTORNEY

(Refer to Important Documents)

Contact information _____

_____

_____

_____

BANK ACCOUNTS

CHECKING ACCOUNT NUMBER:

Bank and routing number _____

_____

Account login and password *(Refer to Account Information)*

_____

_____

SAVINGS ACCOUNT NUMBER:

Bank and routing number _____

_____

Account login and password _____

_____

DEBIT CARD:

Bank _____

Account number _____

PIN _____

CREDIT CARD(S):

Account number(s) _____

_____

Credit card logins and passwords *(Refer to Account Information)*

_____

_____

_____

Details _____

_____

_____

INVESTMENT(S)

Description

ACCOUNT NUMBER(S) _____

_____

_____

CONTACT(S) _____

_____

_____

NOTES _____

_____

_____

OTHER ACCOUNTS

Description

ACCOUNT NUMBER(S) _____

_____

CONTACT(S) _____

_____

_____

NOTES _____

_____

_____

TAX RECORDS

RECORDS LOCATION *(Refer to Important Documents)*

_____

_____

TAX ACCOUNTANT AND CONTACT INFORMATION

_____

_____

_____

WHAT I OWE

MORTGAGE _____

Lender name and contact information _____

_____

_____

Account number _____

Location of documents

PROPERTY TAX INFORMATION

HOME LOAN _____

_____

Lender name and contact information _____

_____

_____

Account number _____

Location of papers

VEHICLE LOAN _____

_____

Lender name and contact information _____

_____

_____

Account number _____

Location of papers

STUDENT LOAN(S) _____

_____

Lender name(s) and contact information _____

_____

_____

Account number(s) _____

_____

Location of papers

MEDICAL BILLS _____

_____

Facility name(s) and contact information _____

_____

_____

Account number(s) _____

_____

> **Location of papers**

CREDIT CARD BILLS _____

_____

Bank name(s) and contact information _____

_____

_____

Account number(s) _____

_____

> **Location of papers**

PERSONAL LOAN(S) _____

_____

Name(s) and contact information _____

_____

_____

Account number(s) _____

_____

Location of papers

LEGAL JUDGMENTS _____

_____

Contact information _____

_____

_____

Account number(s) _____

_____

Location of papers

POSSESSIONS OWED TO OTHERS _____

_____

Details _____

_____

_____

Contact information _____

_____

_____

Location of papers

OTHER _____

_____

_____

_____

OWED TO ME

PERSONAL LOAN(S) _____

_____

Contact information _____

_____

_____

Details _____

_____

_____

_____

_____

Location of papers

JUDGMENTS _____

_____

Contact information _____

_____

_____

Details _____

_____

_____

_____

Location of papers

POSSESSIONS OWED TO ME

Details _____

_____

_____

Contact information _____

_____

Location of papers

OTHER _____

_____

_____

_____

UTILITY BILLS AND ACCOUNTS

GAS COMPANY:

Contact information _____

_____

Account number _____

Account login and password _____

_____

WATER COMPANY:

Contact information _____

_____

Account number _____

Account login and password _____

_____

SEWAGE COMPANY:

Contact information _____

_____

Account number _____

Account login and password _____

_____

POWER COMPANY:

Contact information _____

_____

Account number _____

Account login and password _____

_____

CABLE COMPANY:

Contact information _____

_____

Account number _____

Account login and password _____

_____

INTERNET COMPANY:

Contact information _____

_____

Account number _____

Account login and password _____

_____

PHONE COMPANY:

Contact information _____

_____

Account number _____

Account login and password _____

_____

SUBSCRIPTION:

Contact information _____

_____

Account number _____

Account login(s) and password(s) _____

_____

SUBSCRIPTION:

Contact information _____

_____

Account number _____

Account login(s) and password(s) _____

_____

SUBSCRIPTION:

Contact information _____

_____

Account number _____

Account login(s) and password(s) _____

_____

FINANCIAL

SUBSCRIPTION:

Contact information _____

_____

Account number _____

Account login(s) and password(s) _____

_____

SUBSCRIPTION:

Contact information _____

_____

Account number _____

Account login(s) and password(s) _____

_____

AMAZON:

Account login and password _____

_____

Notes

MEMBERSHIP:

Details _____

Account logins and passwords _____

_____

MEMBERSHIP:

Details _____

Account logins and passwords _____

_____

MEMBERSHIP:

Details _____

Account logins and passwords _____

_____

MEMBERSHIP:

Details _____

Account logins and passwords _____

_____

MEMBERSHIP:

Details _____

Account logins and passwords _____

_____

MEMBERSHIP:

Details _____

Account logins and passwords _____

FINANCIAL

PERSONAL PROPERTY

The following section is one that, while often overlooked in end-of-life planning, can be some of the most important information to pass along to those you leave behind. It's crucial to tell loved ones where they can find not only your will but other documents, keepsakes, and details regarding your property that are often left out of legal documents. Once more though, this planner acts as a guidepost, and what you write here does not grant legal authority for your wishes.

HOUSING

PRIMARY RESIDENCE ADDRESS _____

_____

_____

Co-owner(s) _____

Location of legal documents *(Refer to Important Documents)*

Location of keys _____

_____

Location of furnishing/appliance warranties, maintenance contracts, etc.

_____

_____

Home security company contact information _____

_____

ADDITIONAL RESIDENCE ADDRESS _____

_____

_____

Co-owner(s) _____

_____

Location of legal documents

Location of keys _____

_____

Location of furnishing/appliance warranties, maintenance contracts, etc.

_____

_____

Home security company contact information _____

_____

RENTAL PROPERTIES AND ADDRESSES _____

_____

_____

Co-owner(s) _____

_____

Rental agreement location

Location of furnishing/appliance warranties, maintenance contracts, etc.

_____

_____

Home security company contact information _____

_____

COMMERCIAL PROPERTY ADDRESS _____

_____

_____

Co-owner(s) _____

_____

Location of legal documents

Location of keys _____

_____

VEHICLE(S):

VIN/ID:

Location of keys _____

Location of title *(Refer to Important Documents)*

Location of lease/loan information _____

_____

Insurance information *(Refer to Important Documents)* _____

_____

VIN/ID:

Location of keys _____

Location of title *(Refer to Important Documents)*

Location of lease/loan information _____

_____

Insurance information _(Refer to Important Documents)_ _____

_____

NOTES _____

_____

_____

_____

_____

STORAGE UNIT(S)

COMPANY NAME _____

Unit location(s) _____

_____

Contact information _____

Unit number(s) _____

_____

Location of key(s) _____

_____

NOTES ABOUT CONTENTS

FIREARMS

ITEM(S) _____

_____

_____

LOCATION _____

_____

REGISTRATION INFORMATION _____

_____

_____

PERMIT INFORMATION _____

_____

_____

NOTES _____

_____

_____

VALUABLES AND ITEMS OF SENTIMENTAL VALUE

ITEM:

Location _____

_____

Notes and special instructions _____

_____

ITEM:

Location _____

_____

Notes and special instructions _____

_____

ITEM:

Location _____

_____

Notes and special instructions _____

_____

ITEM:

Location _____

_____

Notes and special instructions _____

_____

ITEM:

Location _____

_____

Notes and special instructions _____

_____

PROPERTY

BUSINESS INFORMATION

This section applies for those who own a business or act as an independent contractor. If you haven't considered what will happen to your business at the time of your passing, I would recommend making those plans with your attorney and any relevant partners who would be taking over for you. This space is not meant to provide detailed plans for the business but simply to allow for your loved ones to know how to coordinate with your business after you pass and how to separate your personal estate from your business estate.

BUSINESS NAME _____

_____

CONTACT INFORMATION _____

_____

_____

LOCATION _____

_____

_____

LANDLORD, EMPLOYEES, ETC. _____

_____

_____

_____

_____

_____

BUSINESS ACCOUNTANT _____

_____

ATTORNEY _____

_____

INSURANCE _____

_____

BANK/CREDIT CARD _____

_____

CUSTOMERS _____

_____

_____

_____

_____

UTILITIES _____

_____

_____

_____

WEBSITES AND SOCIAL MEDIA

INSURANCE INFORMATION

While items like homeowner's insurance may not be the first thing to come to mind while making final preparations, it is still very useful to have this type of information in one place as a guidepost for those left behind. This section's goal is to assist in getting started with transferring or canceling insurance policies as needed.

LIFE INSURANCE

AGENCY/AGENT NAME _____

_____

CONTACT INFORMATION _____

_____

_____

_____

_____

_____

POLICY NUMBER _____

HOMEOWNER'S INSURANCE

AGENCY/AGENT NAME _____

_____

CONTACT INFORMATION _____

_____

_____

POLICY NUMBER _____

RENTAL OR STORAGE INSURANCE

AGENCY/AGENT NAME _____

_____

CONTACT INFORMATION _____

_____

_____

POLICY NUMBER _____

HEALTH INSURANCE

AGENCY/AGENT NAME _____

_____

CONTACT INFORMATION _____

_____

_____

POLICY NUMBER _____

62

VEHICLE INSURANCE

AGENCY/AGENT NAME _____

_____

CONTACT INFORMATION _____

_____

_____

POLICY NUMBER _____

OTHER INSURANCE

AGENCY/AGENT NAME _____

_____

CONTACT INFORMATION _____

_____

_____

POLICY NUMBER _____

OTHER INSURANCE

AGENCY/AGENT NAME _____

_____

CONTACT INFORMATION _____

_____

_____

POLICY NUMBER _____

INFORMATION ABOUT MY BENEFICIARIES

Depending on your life's circumstances, you may have one or more policies that are set up to directly benefit those left behind. A named beneficiary will have a legal right to whatever is set aside for them, policy depending. Let this section assist in either laying out what you currently have in place to more easily navigate once you are gone or considering what you may still need to set up.

LIFE INSURANCE POLICIES

TYPE _____

Account number _____

Amount _____

Beneficiary _____

Location of papers/information

EMPLOYER BENEFITS

BENEFICIARY _____

Location of papers/information

SOCIAL SECURITY

ACCOUNT NUMBER _____

Location of papers/information

RETIREMENT [401(K), PENSION, ETC.]

NAME _____

Account number _____

Contact information _____

_____

Location of papers/information

VETERAN'S BENEFITS

BENEFICIARY _____

Location of papers/information

OTHER BENEFITS

BENEFICIARY _____

Location of papers/information

OTHER BENEFITS

BENEFICIARY _____

Location of papers/information

DEVICES AND ACCOUNTS

When you pass, you may want your loved ones to have access to your computer and devices so that they may enter your important online accounts, such as email and banking. This section is intended for you to leave particular instructions about your accounts, including social media.

Take care to leave someone in charge of these accounts, and make sure they're aware of what you'd like them to do. Giving someone the opportunity to access your accounts goes beyond just personal preference. It's important to deactivate or secure accounts that will no longer be in use to ensure that your personal information is kept private. Additionally, you may want to consider saving important favorite photos, emails, etc., in a secure file to ensure they are kept after your passing.

Regardless of what you decide to do with your accounts, just make sure you clearly outline what you'd like done. It may be a good idea to read any deactivation or deletion policies or even download or save a copy of whatever information is on that account so that others may reference it later.

COMPUTER

LOCATION _____

LOGIN AND PASSWORD _____

_____

Warranty and other information

OTHER DEVICES (PHONES, TABLETS, ETC.)

LOCATION(S) _____

LOGIN(S) AND PASSWORD(S) _____

_____

_____

_____

_____

_____

_____

Warranty and other information

70

EMAIL ACCOUNT #1

USERNAME AND PASSWORD _____

NOTES AND WISHES _____

_____

EMAIL ACCOUNT #2

USERNAME AND PASSWORD _____

NOTES AND WISHES _____

_____

EMAIL ACCOUNT #3

USERNAME AND PASSWORD _____

NOTES AND WISHES _____

_____

EMAIL ACCOUNT #4

USERNAME AND PASSWORD _____

NOTES AND WISHES _____

_____

EMAIL ACCOUNT #5

USERNAME AND PASSWORD _____

NOTES AND WISHES _____

_____

SOCIAL MEDIA ACCOUNT #1:

USERNAME AND PASSWORD _____

_____

NOTES AND WISHES _____

_____

_____

SOCIAL MEDIA ACCOUNT #2:

USERNAME AND PASSWORD _____

_____

NOTES AND WISHES _____

_____

_____

SOCIAL MEDIA ACCOUNT #3:

USERNAME AND PASSWORD _____

_____

NOTES AND WISHES _____

_____

_____

SOCIAL MEDIA ACCOUNT #4:

USERNAME AND PASSWORD _____

_____

NOTES AND WISHES _____

_____

_____

SOCIAL MEDIA ACCOUNT #5:

USERNAME AND PASSWORD _____

_____

NOTES AND WISHES _____

_____

_____

SOCIAL MEDIA ACCOUNT #6:

USERNAME AND PASSWORD _____

_____

NOTES AND WISHES _____

_____

_____

PETS

After you pass, you'll want to ensure your beloved pets are still receiving the best care and support possible. This section should capture all necessary information regarding their care and future custodians as well as any special care needs for your animal companions.

PET NAME:

BREED _____

MEDICAL HISTORY _____

VET CARE ADDRESS _____

_____

VET CARE PHONE NUMBER _____

WHO WILL BE TAKING CARE OF THE PET _____

_____

Special care notes

PET NAME:

BREED _____

MEDICAL HISTORY _____

VET CARE ADDRESS _____

_____

VET CARE PHONE NUMBER _____

WHO WILL BE TAKING CARE OF THE PET _____

_____

Special care notes

PET NAME:

BREED _____

MEDICAL HISTORY _____

VET CARE ADDRESS _____

_____

VET CARE PHONE NUMBER _____

WHO WILL BE TAKING CARE OF THE PET _____

_____

Special care notes

PET NAME:

BREED _____

MEDICAL HISTORY _____

VET CARE ADDRESS _____

_____

VET CARE PHONE NUMBER _____

WHO WILL BE TAKING CARE OF THE PET _____

_____

Special care notes

PET NAME:

BREED _____

MEDICAL HISTORY _____

VET CARE ADDRESS _____

_____

VET CARE PHONE NUMBER _____

WHO WILL BE TAKING CARE OF THE PET _____

_____

Special care notes

PETS

IMPORTANT DOCUMENTS

This section serves as a quick reference point for the locations of any important documents ranging from your birth certificate to your tax records. Filling this section out and ensuring that documents can be reliably found at these locations will ensure that your loved ones have an easy time finding everything they need.

SAFE LOCATION _____

Safe code/access details _____

SAFETY DEPOSIT BOX LOCATION _____

Box number _____

Key location _____

_____

BIRTH CERTIFICATE LOCATION _____

SOCIAL SECURITY CARD LOCATION _____

PASSPORT LOCATION _____

DRIVER'S LICENSE LOCATION _____

MARRIAGE CERTIFICATE LOCATION _____

DIVORCE PAPER LOCATION _____

DEED/RENTAL AGREEMENT LOCATION _____

VEHICLE TITLE LOCATION _____

Registration location _____

Insurance card/policy location _____

LIVING WILL LOCATION _____

HEALTHCARE POWER OF ATTORNEY LOCATION

_____

DNR ORDER LOCATION _____

FINANCIAL POWER OF ATTORNEY LOCATION _____

_____

FUNERAL/BURIAL POLICY LOCATION _____

_____

TAX RECORDS LOCATION _____

COMPUTER DOCUMENTS OF IMPORTANCE _____

_____

ADDRESS BOOK _____

OTHER _____

_____

_____

_____

_____

_____

_____

_____

LAST WISHES

———————

Perhaps the most important section of this planner, the space provided here is intended to capture what other documents cannot: your final message to loved ones. Use this space to note any last words or personal desires at the time of your passing.

MY WISHES

_____

_____

_____

_____

_____

_____

_____

_____

_____

_____

_____

_____

_____

PARTING WORDS

Published by Sourcebooks
P.O. Box 4410, Naperville, Illinois 60567-4410
(630) 961-3900
sourcebooks.com

Printed and bound in China.
OGP 10 9 8 7 6 5 4 3 2 1